Tell Me Your Life Story Dad

A guided journal

and keepsake book

to capture

dad's life story

and memories.

Olek Modoc

Author's Note

Tell Me Your Life Story, Dad
Discovering the depths of your father's story
"Tell Me Your Life Story, Dad" is a touching invitation to uncover the hidden chapters of your father's remarkable life. This engaging guided journal contains 13 reflective chapters, leading you through his early memories, significant life events, and cherished moments. With over 170 prompts, it's a journey of discovery, connection, and legacy.

Searching for the ideal gift? "Tell Me Your Life Story, Dad" is a heartfelt and meaningful present for birthdays, Father's Day, or any special occasion. Offer the gift of connection and memories, allowing your father to share his life story in his own words, creating a precious keepsake for both of you.

Pages to Fill: Populate the journal with your father's stories, memories, and wisdom. Explore every aspect of his childhood, relationships, career, and more. Treasure the handwritten notes and reflections that will become beloved family heirlooms.

Unlock the extraordinary chapters of your father's life and create a lasting legacy that will be cherished for generations. Delve into his experiences, celebrate his successes, and honor the man who shaped your world. Let his voice resonate through the pages of "Tell Me Your Life Story, Dad."

With Love,
Olek

TABLE OF CONTENTS

"A father's job is not to teach his children how to be like him, but to teach them to be better than him." - Unknown

INTRODUCTION

This journal was created exclusively for you, allowing you to embark on an exciting journey of discovery and connection with your dad. It serves as a gateway to explore his life story through engaging prompts and thought-provoking questions. Get ready to unveil the fascinating chapters of your dad's life and strengthen your bond along the way.

Uncover Your Dad's Story:

Inside these pages, you'll find a treasure trove of experiences, memories, and adventures waiting to be shared. By hearing your dad's story, you'll gain a deeper understanding of who he is as a person and the remarkable journey that has shaped him. Prepare to be inspired, entertained, and enlightened as you navigate the chapters of his life.

This journal is your key to unlock a world of stories and insights from your dad's life. Use the prompts as conversation starters to delve into his past, from his childhood adventures to his memorable milestones. Engage in meaningful discussions, listen attentively, and cherish the moments as you uncover the unique tapestry of your dad's experiences.

Get ready for an extraordinary voyage through your dad's life story.

This journal is your passport to creating lasting memories, strengthening your bond, and gaining valuable insights from the remarkable person who is your dad. Enjoy this incredible adventure together and embrace the power of storytelling as you uncover the extraordinary tale of your dad's life. Let the journey begin!

"A dad is a son's first hero and a daughter's first love, but he is also a lifelong friend." - Unknown

My Details

MY NAME: _____

DATE OF BIRTH: _____

BIRTH PLACE: _____

HEIGHT: _____

EYE COLOR: _____

AGE: _____

WEIGHT: _____

HAIR COLOR: _____

ATTACH YOUR BABY PHOTO HERE

Time Capsule

TODAY'S DATE:_____

POPULATION OF YOUR COUNTRY:_____

POPULATION OF THE WORLD:_____

LEADER OF YOUR COUNTRY:_____

The average cost of these items

BOTTLE OF MILK:_____

CUP OF COFFEE:_____

BAR OF CHOCOLATE:_____

1 LITRE OF DISEAL:_____

MAGAZINE:_____

BOOK:_____

PASTAGE STAMP:_____

NEWSPAPER:_____

A HOUSE:_____

CAR:_____

"A father's presence and guidance can be
the greatest gift a child receives." - Unknown

"A dad is someone who holds you when you cry, scolds you when you break the rules, shines with pride when you succeed, and has faith in you even when you fail." - Unknown

IT'S YOUR BIRTHDAY

What is your birthdate?

_____

_____

What was your full name at birth?

_____

Were you born in a hospital, If not, where?

_____

_____

_____

In which city were you born?

_____

_____

How old were your parents when you were born?

_____

_____

Did you do anything funny when you were born?

_____

_____

_____

_____

IT'S YOUR BIRTHDAY

How did your parents describe you as a baby?

_____

_____

_____

_____

_____

Did you have any nicknames as a child?

_____

_____

What were your first words?

_____

_____

_____

How old were you when started to walk?

_____

_____

_____

IT'S YOUR BIRTHDAY

When you were a little child, how did your family make your birthday feel extra special?

_____

_____

_____

_____

_____

When it's your birthday, who are the special people you love to spend it with?

_____

_____

Were there any particular games or activities that your family would organize for your birthday celebrations?

_____

_____

_____

_____

_____

IT'S YOUR BIRTHDAY

Describe the decorations your family would put up to celebrate your birthday.

_____

_____

_____

_____

_____

_____

_____

Were there any specific birthday traditions or rituals that your family followed each year?

_____

_____

_____

_____

_____

_____

_____

_____

IT'S YOUR BIRTHDAY

Were there any surprises or pranks that your family would play on your birthday?

_____

_____

_____

_____

_____

_____

_____

Describe a memorable birthday gift you received as a child from your family. What made it special?

_____

_____

_____

_____

_____

_____

_____

IT'S YOUR BIRTHDAY

What were some of the traditional foods or treats your family prepared for your birthday?

_____

_____

_____

_____

_____

_____

_____

Were there any specific birthday traditions or rituals that your family followed each year?

_____

_____

_____

_____

_____

_____

_____

IT'S YOUR BIRTHDAY

Did your family have any unique songs or chants that they would sing for you on your birthday?

_____

_____

_____

_____

_____

Reflecting on your childhood birthdays, what do you think your family's birthday celebrations taught you about love, family, or the importance of marking special occasions?

_____

_____

_____

_____

_____

_____

_____

_____

EARLY CHILDHOOD

Who was your best childhood friend? Write about some of the fun things you used to do together.

_____

_____

_____

_____

_____

_____

_____

_____

_____

_____

_____

_____

_____

_____

EARLY CHILDHOOD

Describe one of your earliest childhood memories.
How old were you? What bits and pieces can you recall?

_____

_____

_____

_____

_____

_____

_____

_____

_____

_____

_____

_____

_____

_____

EARLY CHILDHOOD

During your early childhood, what was your favorite toy or object that you treasured the most?

_____

_____

_____

Describe the house or neighborhood where you spent your early childhood. What are some vivid memories that come to mind?

_____

_____

_____

_____

_____

_____

_____

_____

_____

_____

_____

EARLY CHILDHOOD

When you were little, did you ever try to run away from home?
What made you want to leave? What did you pack? How far did you get?

_____

_____

_____

_____

_____

_____

Describe a game or activity you used to play with a sibling.

_____

_____

_____

_____

_____

_____

EARLY CHILDHOOD

Were you shy as a child? Bossy? Obnoxious? Describe several of your childhood character traits. How did those qualities show themselves? Are you still that way today?

_____

_____

_____

_____

_____

What childhood memories of your mother and father do you have? Describe a couple of snapshot moments.

_____

_____

_____

_____

_____

_____

_____

_____

EARLY CHILDHOOD

Describe the most unusual or memorable place you have lived.

_____

_____

_____

_____

_____

_____

_____

_____

Do you have quirky or interesting relatives on your family tree?
Describe one or two of them.

_____

_____

_____

_____

_____

_____

_____

EARLY CHILDHOOD

Were there any specific activities or games that you enjoyed with your friends during your early childhood?

_____

_____

_____

_____

_____

_____

_____

_____

Recall a funny or mischievous incident from your early childhood that still brings a smile to your face when you think about it.

_____

_____

_____

_____

_____

_____

_____

EARLY CHILDHOOD

What were some of your favorite books, movies, or cartoons that captivated your imagination and played a role in your early childhood?

_____

_____

_____

_____

_____

_____

_____

_____

Did you grow up with family traditions? Describe one.

_____

_____

_____

_____

_____

EARLY CHILDHOOD

Reflecting on your early childhood, how would you describe the overall atmosphere or ambiance of your family home? What made it unique or special?

THE SCHOOL YEARS

Describe your earliest memories of starting school. How did you feel on your first day?

_____

_____

_____

_____

_____

_____

_____

_____

_____

_____

_____

_____

_____

THE SCHOOL YEARS

What was your favorite elementary school memory and why was it special?

_____

_____

_____

_____

_____

_____

_____

_____

_____

_____

_____

_____

_____

THE SCHOOL YEARS

How was middle school or junior high different from elementary school for you?

_____

_____

_____

_____

_____

_____

Who was your favorite high school teacher or subject and why?

_____

_____

_____

_____

_____

_____

_____

_____

_____

THE SCHOOL YEARS

What grades did you get in high school?

_____

_____

_____

_____

_____

_____

Who were your closest friends during your school years?
What adventures or mischief did you get up to together?

_____

_____

_____

_____

_____

_____

_____

_____

_____

THE SCHOOL YEARS

How did you navigate friendships and social dynamics during your school years? Were there any notable friendships or conflicts?

_____

_____

_____

_____

_____

_____

Did you have a favorite teacher or mentor who made a significant impact on your life? Tell us about them.

_____

_____

_____

_____

_____

_____

_____

_____

THE SCHOOL YEARS

Share a funny or interesting anecdote from your school years that still makes you laugh or smile.

THE SCHOOL YEARS

Did you participate in any extracurricular activities or clubs?

_____

_____

_____

_____

_____

_____

_____

_____

_____

_____

_____

_____

_____

_____

THE SCHOOL YEARS

Recall a particularly challenging subject or assignment during your school years. How did you overcome it?

_____

_____

_____

_____

_____

What subjects or areas of study were you most passionate about during your school years? Why did they resonate with you?

_____

_____

_____

_____

_____

_____

_____

_____

_____

THE SCHOOL YEARS

How did your school years contribute to your personal growth and development? What valuable lessons did you learn during that time?

_____

_____

_____

_____

_____

_____

_____

_____

_____

_____

_____

_____

_____

_____

THE TEENAGE YEARS

Could you describe your typical morning routine during that time?

_____

_____

_____

_____

_____

_____

_____

_____

Were you usually punctual, late, or early? What did this reveal about your personality or habits?

_____

_____

_____

_____

_____

THE TEENAGE YEARS

What were some of your favorite activities or things you enjoyed doing with your friends?

_____

_____

_____

_____

_____

_____

_____

_____

_____

_____

_____

_____

_____

THE TEENAGE YEARS

Were there any specific fashion trends or music genres that were populat during your teenage years? How did they influence your style or interests?

_____

_____

_____

_____

_____

_____

_____

_____

Describe a favorite food or dish that you loved. What made it special to you?

_____

_____

_____

_____

_____

THE TEENAGE YEARS

Can you recall a time when you did something really special or kind for someone? Share that experience with us.

_____

_____

_____

_____

_____

_____

_____

Who in your life were you most grateful for, and why?

_____

_____

_____

_____

_____

THE TEENAGE YEARS

In your younger years, what was the greatest responsibility your parents entrusted you with? How did you handle it?

_____

_____

_____

_____

_____

_____

_____

_____

Can you share a story about someone who influenced or changed your perspective back then?

_____

_____

_____

_____

_____

_____

THE TEENAGE YEARS

Share a cherished memory from one of your summer vacations.
What made it so memorable?

_____

_____

_____

_____

_____

_____

_____

_____

_____

_____

_____

_____

_____

_____

_____

THE TEENAGE YEARS

Were you good at keeping secrets? Why or why not? How did you approach confidentiality?

_____

_____

_____

_____

_____

_____

_____

_____

_____

Did you ever have to have a difficult conversation with someone? How did you handle it? What did you learn from the experience?

_____

_____

_____

_____

_____

_____

THE TEENAGE YEARS

Share a funny or embarrassing moment from your teenage years that you can look back on now with a sense of humor.

_____

_____

_____

_____

_____

_____

_____

How did technology and the internet impact your teenage years? Share any memorable experiences or how it influenced your social life.

_____

_____

_____

_____

_____

THE TEENAGE YEARS

Did you pray? Why or why not? How did spirituality or faith play a role in your life back then?

_____

_____

_____

_____

_____

_____

_____

_____

What was your favorite book? How did it impact or influence you at that time?

_____

_____

_____

_____

_____

THE TEENAGE YEARS

Reflecting on your teenage years, what are some life lessons or values that you developed during that time? How have they shaped you as an adult?

_____

_____

_____

_____

_____

_____

_____

_____

_____

_____

_____

_____

_____

_____

EDUCATION AND CAREER

What did you study and where?

_____

_____

_____

_____

_____

_____

_____

_____

What field are you currently working in, and what is your role?

_____

_____

_____

_____

_____

_____

EDUCATION AND CAREER

Share an accomplishment or milestone in your education or career that you're proud of.

_____

_____

_____

_____

_____

_____

_____

_____

What do you think would have been better for you in your career?

_____

_____

_____

_____

_____

_____

EDUCATION AND CAREER

Describe a person or mentor who has had a significant impact on your current educational or professional journey.

_____

_____

_____

_____

_____

_____

_____

_____

Can you explain why you believed it was important to learn to read?

_____

_____

_____

_____

_____

EDUCATION AND CAREER

What careers seemed interesting to you back then? Why?

_____

_____

_____

_____

_____

_____

What jobs did you consider as parallel plans back then?
(Plan B, Plan C, etc.)

_____

_____

_____

_____

What career paths were you able to cross off your list?

_____

_____

_____

_____

_____

EDUCATION AND CAREER

Were there any careers that you considered dangerous?

_____

_____

_____

_____

_____

_____

_____

What extracurricular activities did you enjoy? What did you learn
about yourself from participating in those activities?

_____

_____

_____

_____

_____

_____

_____

_____

_____

EDUCATION AND CAREER

If you were guaranteed success, what would you have done?

_____

_____

_____

_____

_____

_____

Can you recall a challenge you faced in your studies or career? How did you overcome it?

_____

_____

_____

_____

_____

_____

_____

_____

EDUCATION AND CAREER

Describe any steps you have taken to align your education and career goals for long-term success.

_____

_____

_____

_____

_____

_____

_____

_____

_____

Share a recent experience where you had to adapt to new technologies or industry trends in your work.

_____

_____

_____

_____

_____

FAMILY TREE

FAMILY TREE

Can you share the names of all your immediate family members?

_____

_____

_____

_____

_____

_____

_____

_____

Describe the special bond you share with your parents or guardians.

_____

_____

_____

_____

_____

FAMILY TREE

Who are your siblings, and what is your relationship like with each of them?

_____

_____

_____

_____

_____

_____

_____

_____

Who were your grandparents? Can you share their names and any special memories you have of them?

_____

_____

_____

_____

_____

_____

FAMILY TREE

Are there any aunts, uncles, or cousins who played a significant role in your life? Tell us about them.

_____

_____

_____

_____

_____

_____

_____

_____

Do you have any nieces, nephews, or younger relatives? How do you enjoy spending time with them?

_____

_____

_____

_____

_____

_____

_____

FAMILY TREE

Who are your closest cousins, and what are some memorable moments you've shared with them?

_____

_____

_____

_____

_____

_____

_____

_____

_____

_____

_____

_____

_____

_____

FAMILY TREE

Are there any family traditions or rituals that have been passed down through generations? Describe one that holds special meaning for you.

Share a story about a family member who overcame significant challenges or achieved great success.

FAMILY TREE

Can you recall any family legends or tales that have been passed down through the generations?

_____

_____

_____

_____

_____

Reflecting on your family tree, are there any surprising or interesting connections to other families or lineages?

_____

_____

_____

_____

_____

_____

_____

RELATIONSHIP & MARRIAGE

Who was your first love, and what was the story behind your relationship?

_____

_____

_____

_____

_____

_____

_____

_____

_____

_____

_____

_____

Who was your longest-lasting relationship before you got married?

_____

_____

_____

RELATIONSHIP & MARRIAGE

What did love mean to you back then?

_____

_____

_____

_____

Who was the last person you said "I love you" to during that time?

_____

_____

How did being in love back then affect your life?

_____

_____

_____

_____

_____

_____

RELATIONSHIP & MARRIAGE

Were you hurt in past relationships? If so, how did i affect you?

_____

_____

_____

_____

_____

_____

_____

_____

How did you communicate loyalty in your relationships?

_____

_____

_____

_____

_____

_____

_____

RELATIONSHIP & MARRIAGE

Did you fight fairly in your relationships?

_____

_____

_____

_____

_____

_____

_____

Which relationships did you respect and admire?

_____

_____

_____

_____

_____

_____

RELATIONSHIP & MARRIAGE

Did you believe in love at first sight?

_____

_____

_____

_____

_____

According to you back then, what was the secret to a great relationship?

_____

_____

_____

_____

_____

_____

_____

_____

RELATIONSHIP & MARRIAGE

How did you meet your wife? Share the story of how your paths crossed.

_____

_____

_____

_____

_____

_____

_____

_____

_____

_____

_____

_____

_____

_____

_____

_____

RELATIONSHIP & MARRIAGE

Can you recall the moment you knew your wife was the one you wanted to spend your life with?

_____

_____

_____

_____

_____

_____

How did you propose to your wife? Share the details of that special moment.

_____

_____

_____

_____

_____

_____

_____

_____

RELATIONSHIP & MARRIAGE

Describe a favorite memory from your wedding day.

_____

_____

_____

_____

_____

_____

_____

_____

_____

_____

_____

_____

_____

_____

RELATIONSHIP & MARRIAGE

How has your relationship with your wife evolved and grown over the years?

_____

_____

_____

_____

_____

_____

_____

Did you feel like there was a need you were not fulfilling for your partner?

_____

_____

_____

_____

_____

_____

_____

_____

RELATIONSHIP & MARRIAGE

10 things that you found special about your partner?

_____

_____

_____

_____

_____

_____

_____

_____

_____

_____

_____

_____

_____

_____

RELATIONSHIP & MARRIAGE

Can you recall any significant challenges you faced as a couple and how they strengthened your bond?

RELATIONSHIP & MARRIAGE

Share a story about a surprise or special gesture you did for your spouse to celebrate your love.

_____

_____

_____

_____

_____

_____

_____

_____

_____

_____

_____

_____

_____

_____

_____

FATHERHOOD

What was your initial reaction when you found out you were going to be a dad?

_____

_____

_____

_____

_____

_____

How did becoming a father change your perspective on life?

_____

_____

_____

_____

_____

_____

_____

_____

FATHERHOOD

Describe a cherished memory from your child's early years.

_____

_____

_____

_____

_____

_____

_____

_____

_____

_____

_____

_____

_____

_____

_____

FATHERHOOD

Share a parenting challenge you faced and how you overcame it.

FATHERHOOD

What values or principles do you strive to instill in your children?

_____

_____

_____

_____

_____

Can you recall a funny or memorable parenting moment that still makes you smile?

_____

_____

_____

_____

_____

_____

_____

_____

_____

FATHERHOOD

Describe the bond you share with each of your children and what makes it special

_____

_____

_____

_____

_____

_____

How do you balance your role as a father with other responsibilities in your life?

_____

_____

_____

_____

_____

_____

_____

_____

_____

_____

FATHERHOOD

Share a valuable lesson you've learned from being a father.

_____

_____

_____

_____

_____

How do you show your love and support to your children on a daily basis?

_____

_____

_____

_____

_____

_____

_____

_____

_____

_____

FATHERHOOD

How do you navigate and handle conflicts or disagreement with you children?

_____

_____

_____

_____

_____

_____

_____

_____

_____

_____

_____

_____

_____

_____

CHALLENGES AND TRIUMPHS

Can you share a significant challenge you faced in your life and how you overcame it?

_____

_____

_____

_____

_____

_____

_____

_____

_____

_____

_____

_____

_____

_____

CHALLENGES AND TRIUMPHS

Describe a moment when you felt a great sense of triumph or accomplishment.

CHALLENGES AND TRIUMPHS

Share a time when you had to step out of your comfort zone and how it impacted your life.

_____

_____

_____

_____

_____

Can you recall a moment when you felt like giving up, but persevered and came out stronger?

_____

_____

_____

_____

_____

_____

_____

_____

CHALLENGES AND TRIUMPHS

Describe a challenging period in your life and how it shaped your character.

CHALLENGES AND TRIUMPHS

Can you recall a time when you had to take a risk and how it turned out?

_____

_____

_____

_____

_____

_____

_____

_____

_____

_____

_____

_____

_____

_____

_____

CHALLENGES AND TRIUMPHS

How did you navigate a difficult relationship or conflict and find resolution?

CHALLENGES AND TRIUMPHS

Describe a triumph or success that you are particularly proud of and why it is significant to you.

_____

_____

_____

_____

_____

_____

_____

_____

_____

_____

_____

_____

_____

_____

REFLECTIONS

In your life, what would you like to be doing one year from now? How about in 10 years?

_____

_____

_____

_____

_____

_____

_____

_____

_____

What are some things you're eagerly anticipating in the future?

_____

_____

_____

_____

_____

REFLECTIONS

Do you feel you possess any standout skills? If so, do you believe you're utilizing them to their fullest potential in your life?

_____

_____

_____

_____

_____

When it comes to enjoying your day, what activities or pursuits bring you the most joy?

_____

_____

_____

_____

_____

_____

_____

_____

REFLECTIONS

Can you share some of the things that never fail to make you laugh and bring a smile to your face?

_____

_____

_____

_____

_____

_____

_____

Reflecting on the people in your life, who are the individuals you consider to be your biggest sources of support and why?

_____

_____

_____

_____

_____

_____

_____

REFLECTIONS

Describe a moment from your life that you will always remember and explain why it holds such significant meaning for you.

REFLECTIONS

If there was one thing you wish more people knew about you, what would it be?

_____

_____

_____

_____

_____

Throughout your life, what are some surprising or unexpected experiences or realizations you've had about life in general?

_____

_____

_____

_____

_____

_____

_____

_____

REFLECTIONS

In your opinion, what is your greatest personal success? And what about your most notable professional accomplishment?

_____

_____

_____

_____

_____

_____

_____

What aspects of life do you find to be particularly fear-inducing or unsettling?

_____

_____

_____

_____

_____

_____

_____

REFLECTIONS

Can you identify and share five things that you genuinely love about yourself?

_____

_____

_____

_____

_____

_____

_____

What is your favorite quote, and what about it resonates with you? What does it signify or mean in your life?

_____

_____

_____

_____

_____

_____

_____

_____

REFLECTIONS

How do you perceive miracles? Have you ever experienced a moment that you would consider miraculous?

_____

_____

_____

_____

_____

_____

Tell me about a secret that you've held onto and have never shared with anyone before.

_____

_____

_____

_____

_____

_____

REFLECTIONS

What are some of the things currently causing frustration in your life? Do you believe there are actions you can take to address them?

_____

_____

_____

_____

_____

_____

_____

If you were given a million dollars that had to be spent within a year, how would you choose to allocate that money?

_____

_____

_____

_____

_____

_____

_____

SHORT QUESTIONS

What's the most embarrassing dad joke you've ever told?

_____

_____

_____

Did you have a questionable fashion phase that you'd rather forget?

_____

_____

_____

Have you accidentally walked into a glass door thinking it was open?

_____

_____

Did you attempt a dance move that went horribly wrong?

_____

_____

_____

Have you mistaken salt for sugar while cooking? How did it taste?

_____

_____

SHORT QUESTIONS

Did you get stuck in a funny or awkward situation that you can't help but laugh about now?

_____

_____

_____

Have you tried to impersonate a famous celebrity? How did it go?

_____

_____

_____

_____

_____

What's the most embarrassing thing you've done to impress a crush?

_____

_____

_____

_____

_____

SHORT QUESTIONS

Have you had a memorable encounter with a wild animal that left you startled?

_____

_____

_____

Did you fall asleep in an unexpected or unusual place?

_____

_____

_____

Have you tried to sing karaoke but forgot the lyrics halfway through?

_____

_____

_____

Did you have a funny misunderstanding due to a language barrier?

_____

_____

_____

_____

SHORT QUESTIONS

Have you pulled a harmless prank on someone that made everyone burst into laughter?

Have you accidentally worn mismatched shoes or socks without realizing it?

Did you unintentionally startle someone and then felt guilty but couldn't stop laughing?

Have you accidentally sent a text message to the wrong person and had to face the consequences?

SHORT QUESTIONS

What's the silliest thing you've done to make your kids laugh?

_____

_____

Have you had a memorable experience with a practical joke or prank played on you?

_____

_____

_____

Did you ever try to pull off a fancy cooking recipe but ended up with a kitchen disaster?

_____

_____

Have you been caught doing something silly or embarrassing by a family member?

_____

_____

_____

_____

SHORT QUESTIONS

Have you ever attempted to breakdance and ended up breaking something instead?

_____

_____

Did you ever accidentally say something hilarious when you thought no one was listening?

_____

_____

_____

What's the most ridiculous excuse you've used to get out of a situation?

_____

_____

_____

_____

_____

_____

SHORT QUESTIONS

What's the weirdest thing you've ever eaten and actually enjoyed?

_____

_____

_____

Did you ever have a misadventure while attempting a DIY project?

_____

_____

_____

_____

_____

_____

What's the most hilarious misunderstanding you've had with a foreign language or accent?

_____

_____

_____

_____

_____

NOTES TO LOVED ONES

NOTES TO LOVED ONES

NOTES TO LOVED ONES

NOTES TO LOVED ONES

NOTES TO LOVED ONES

NOTES TO LOVED ONES

NOTES TO LOVED ONES

NOTES TO LOVED ONES

NOTES TO LOVED ONES

NOTES TO LOVED ONES

Made in the USA
Monee, IL
23 June 2024

60391326R00066